HOW TO PASS THE UK POLICE OFFICER ROLE PLAY / INTERACTIVE EXERCISES

TECHNIQUES AND TACTICS FOR THE SERIOUS CANDIDATE

CJ Benham

Orders: Please contact MoneyTreeMasters – via policecourse@moneytreemasters.co.uk

First Published 2017

ISBN: 9781549959721

Disclaimer: Every effort has been made to ensure the accuracy of the information contained within this study guide at the time of publication. CJ Benham and any of its authors cannot be held responsible for anyone failing any part of any selection process as result of any information contained within this guide. MoneyTreeMasters and any of its team of authors cannot be held responsible for any errors or omissions within this guide, however caused. No responsibility for loss or damage occasioned by any person acting or refraining from action, as a result of the material in this publication can be accepted by MoneyTreeMasters or the author. The information within this guide does not represent the views or opinions of any third party service or organisation.

CONTENTS

This guide is based on the teachings in our new online course that is available at www.moneytreemasters.co.uk

Don't waste £'s or your valuable time attending an <u>expensive one day course</u>. Sit back, relax and gain expert information, at your own pace and with the ability to review and recap all elements of the course 24/7, 365 days a year.

INTRODUCTION

Welcome to your Pass the Process study guide to Passing the UK Police Officer Role Plays. This guide is unlike any other available on the market. It has been designed to utilise specific training principles which focus on RESULTS. The results are based on selection criteria for the specific chapters "modules" that the book has been structured around.

To use this guide most effectively, try not to dip in and out of chapters, work through the guide start to finish and make use of the additional study materials available in the market.

I am sure you are more than aware of how competitive it is to become a UK Police Officer. Interestingly however, this competition is not really focused on your performance versus other candidates, it is based more on your performance against selection criteria defined by the National College of Policing.

The guide has been written in a chronological format, focusing on the Police Officer Interview process. However, some forces are known to take slight variations from this format, in terms of selection process order of running. Please double check with the constabulary you wish to apply for.

The Police Officer Selection Process is not easy to complete, only 5 – 10% of initial applicants are successful on reaching the final stages. With many thousands of people applying for just a few posts, this role has always been a challenge to be recruited for.

Central to this guide is the ethos of our training techniques, these are designed to give you the edge over other candidates and our aim is to help you be successful.

Whilst it would be inappropriate for us to provide you with the exact scoring criteria the Police Service use for assessing candidates, this guide will demonstrate and provide you with key strategies and models to help focus your efforts in every stage of the interview process.

Thank you for purchasing this guide. I trust you will find it useful and informative. Please do leave feedback on your purchase, your views and opinions are important to me. If you want even greater insight, join the course online and set yourself apart from the competition.

Best wishes for your future.

CJ Benham Founder – PassTheProcess & MoneyTreeMasters

PREFACE BY AUTHOR CJ BENHAM

Having served both as a Special Constable and as a "Regular" Police Constable, I understand the pressures these selection processes will place upon you. In fact, being completely honest with you, it took me three attempts to become a regular officer, why? Bad luck, misfortune? Neither, the truth was that despite my abilities and what I believed I needed to demonstrate, particularly at the One Day Assessment Centre, What I thought I needed to do and what was actually required were set out of sync with each other.

Being a Police Officer is an immensely challenging, rewarding, difficult and hugely enjoyable job. No two days are the same, no two events are the same and it is this variety and the fast pace of the role that appeals to many candidates. Some of the training and experiences I gained in the role of a Police Officer, fundamentally changed me as a person, they will you to. This is a truly unique role and one that takes more personal commitment and dedication than most people would realise.

After spending several years as both a Special Constable and Police Officer, I decided that perhaps this role was not right for me, there was something more I was craving and upon reflection, I didn't really enjoy lots of paperwork (there is a huge amount in that role!). I left the force in the early 2000s and sought to expand my professional skill set in other areas.

My career has developed and grown on the foundations the Police Service instilled in me. But nothing is through chance. To me preparation has become a clear defining factor in terms of success and continual improvement. After leaving the Police Service I have held positions in both small and now global companies. The vast proportion of what I now do is in regards to Training and Performance Development. This has opened many doors for me and taken me on exciting journeys into various industries and different countries.

Back in early 2009, I was approached by an expanding provider of careers information guides and ebooks. They were looking for a tutor with a proven ability to provide the best courses for their customers. Since May 2009, I delivered ALL of their training courses which were focused on the recruitment processes for various roles. This includes amongst others, Police Officer, Firefighter, Paramedic, Train Driver, Magistrate, Army/Navy/RAF Officers. The number of people I have personally trained on these courses now reaches well in excess of 3500.

I have a firm belief that nothing should be left to chance and that true training focuses on the resulting behaviors from the delegate.

What does this mean?

Just providing information will enable some delegates to gain success, but it won't empower all to go away from a training course with strategies or reproducible techniques, that are proven to meet the requirements of the potential employer.

Please work through this guide from the very beginning to the end, despite what you may already know about the Police Selection Process. If you really want the edge over other candidates, then please take some time to reflect on how understanding the models and strategies enclosed can set you apart from others.

CHAPTER 1 THE ROLE OF A UK POLICE OFFICER

I t is extremely important that you have a full understanding of the role of a Police Officer before you begin the application process. Many people's perception of the job role is based on the influence of media and television. Unfortunately, this is slightly skewed as many aspects of a Police Officers role don't make entertaining or pleasant viewing. Rest assured there are some big highs well as big lows in this role, it's not all fast cars, foot chases and catching bad guys. There are many elements and day to day tasks which balance out the adrenaline fueled bursts of activity.

A Police Constable is the frontline of the criminal justice system and community engagement. They will operate under general supervision, but will also be placed into scenarios where operating independently is essential. As a Police Officer you are responsible for the protection of life and property, the prevention and detection of crime and the maintenance of public order through a range of sworn powers in line with the Police Services organisational standards.

As a Constable you must be able to gather and submit information that has the potential to support law enforcement objectives. You will provide an initial response to incidents including Public Order or Road Traffic Collisions (RTCs). Through the provisions of powers given to you, your day will also include arresting, detaining or reporting individuals to Court. You will conduct priority and volume investigations which involves many differing types of techniques. As such, you will also be asked to interview victims and witnesses in relation to priority and volume investigations. Interviewing suspects in relation to priority and volume investigations is also a regular activity as you begin to build cases and investigate crime. Quite often you will search individuals and their personal property for evidence, weapons and controlled substances. Searching also includes carrying out systematic searches of vehicles, premises and open areas.

A huge part of your role is to manage conflict and being able to diffuse conflict is paramount to your success in potentially volatile situations. Police Officers also provide initial support to victims, survivors and witnesses and assess their need for further support from both the Police Service and other agencies.

Every day will present you with new challenges, different situations and unique events to deal with. Police Constables are the front line officers in the UK Police Service and nearly three quarters of all Police Officer in England and Wales hold the rank of Constable. Until very recently, all Police Officers started out in the rank of Constable before progressing up the command chain.

One you join, you will embark on a two year Probationary period in which you will be faced with differing tasks and types of training. Below is an example of a probationers schedule for the first two years of their police career.

Internal training – 10 weeks

During this period students will be taught a number of both legislative and practical skills which will give them the opportunity to develop the knowledge already learned at College or University.

This includes operationally based and assessed role plays, an interview skills course and opportunities to work in the community as well as a number of lessons from experienced Police Officers in areas vital in their role as a Constable.

Please note that the training course consists of 1 week of induction followed by 10 weeks of internal training.

Normally during the 10 weeks initial training you will not be able to take annual leave.

IT Training – 2 weeks

For those new staff who have never worked within the Police in another capacity this is an opportunity to learn the computer systems that are used by the relevant constabulary and also includes a period of leave.

Tutoring Phase – 10 weeks

Once a probationary Officer's trainers are satisfied that they have adequately passed the above courses they will be released to the 'Street Duties Tutoring Unit'.

This unit has a number of experienced Tutor Constables around the County who will work with new staff to develop their skills yet further in an operational environment. Working on either a 1-1 or 1-2 basis they will deal with day to day incidents on Response teams, have an opportunity to work with local Neighbourhood teams and also to carry out interviews and low level investigations, until the tutor Constable is satisfied that the probationer is suitable for independent patrol status allowing them to work alone.

Independent Patrol Status

Once independent patrol status is achieved Students will be asked to complete a Level 3 Diploma in Policing which is designed to evidence that Probationary Officers have the skills necessary to perform at an acceptable standard as a Constable.

This period runs up to two years during which students will be supported by a PC Assessor and will have regular meetings to evidence their achievement and in order that the Assessor can identify where they need to focus their attention.

Response Strand attachment – 12 weeks

Students will first be attached to the Response strand on a Targeted Patrol Team. This will give new Constables an opportunity to work shifts with a rota developing their skills and to start toward their Diploma.

Investigation Strand attachment – 11 weeks

During an eleven week period between weeks 34 and 56 students will be given the opportunity to develop in the Investigation Strand. This will give them an opportunity to investigate crimes and carry out interviews as well as learning more about the role of a CID team.

Neighbourhood Strand attachment – 11 weeks

During an eleven week period between weeks 34 and 56 students will be given the opportunity to develop in the Neighbourhood Strand. Understanding local issues, becoming involved in community meetings and dealing with Anti Social behaviour and problems, Constables will get an insight into Neighbourhood Policing in Surrey.

During this period Probationers will also carry out a short attachment in the Tasking and Coordination Strand in order to understand their role in the force.

56 Weeks – 2 Years

At the 56 weeks stage Constables should in most cases have experienced all areas of the business and completed their Level 3 Diploma in Policing.

At this point, having given preferences to Human Resources in recent weeks and depending on the need of Strands across the Force Constables will be given their permanent posting.

2 Years – Confirmation

At the 2 year point and assuming that students have met the required standard they will be confirmed in appointment in the Office of Constable.

Congratulations, at this point you are now a fully confirmed Police Constable!

CHAPTER 2 THE POLICE OFFICER CORE COMPETENCY REQUIREMENTS

I n October 2013 the National Policing Improvements Agency (now defunct and replaced by the College of Policing) released six new Police Officer Core Competency requirements. These are key skills and abilities that have been determined as to what makes a good Police Officer. The six Core Competencies are:

Serving the Public

Openness to Change

Service Delivery

Professionalism

Decision Making

Working with Others

If you are going to increase your chances of success in the selection process, then having a full understanding of these and what they mean to potential candidates is essential.

Below is the full description of each Core Competency:

Serving the public

- Demonstrates a real belief in public service, focusing on what matters to the public and will best serve their interests.
- Understands the expectations, changing needs and concerns of different communities, and strives to address them.
- Builds public confidence by talking with people in local communities to explore their viewpoints and break down barriers between them and the police.
- Understands the impact and benefits of policing for different communities, and identifies the best way to deliver services to them.

- Works in partnership with other agencies to deliver the best possible overall service to the public.

Serving the public is all about, great customer service but also being able to approach all members of the community and being able to build bridges and reach out to them. Here the Police Service are looking for you to be able to demonstrate how well you are able to look after people, give great customer focus and be willing to engage with the whole community.

Openness to change

- Positive about change, adapting rapidly to different ways of working and putting effort into making them work.
- Flexible and open to alternative approaches to solving problems.
- Finds better, more cost-effective ways to do things, making suggestions for change and putting forward ideas for improvement.
- Takes an innovative and creative approach to solving problems.

Openness to change is a completely new direction for the Police Service. Today's modern Police Service is still largely inefficient and is going to need to adapt as time goes by. What the Police Service are looking to establish with this Core Competency, is that you are the type of candidate who will be flexible in your approach to situations, adapt and be positive about organisational change and be willing to work through those changes, being loyal and committed to the cause.

Service delivery

- Understands the organisation's objectives and priorities, and how own work fits into these.
- Plans and organises tasks effectively, taking a structured and methodical approach to achieving outcomes.
- Manages multiple tasks effectively by thinking things through in advance, prioritising and managing time well.
- Focuses on the outcomes to be achieved, working quickly and accurately and seeking guidance when appropriate.

Service delivery is focusing on you delivering the best value for money whilst completing your role as a Police Officer. The Police Service is paid for by the community, as such, we want the best possible service for our investment. This relates to the phrase of "proactive policing" whereby you will not be the type of person to arrive on duty to "see what happens". Here they are looking for you to demonstrate how you take a structured and methodical approach to your work to gain the best return.

Professionalism

- Acts with integrity, in line with the values and ethical standards of the Police Service.
- Takes ownership for resolving problems, demonstrating courage and resilience in dealing with difficult and potentially volatile situations.
- Acts on own initiative to address issues, showing a strong work ethic and demonstrating extra effort when required.
- Upholds professional standards, acting honestly and ethically, and challenges unprofessional conduct or discriminatory behaviour.
- Asks for and acts on feedback, learning from experience and developing own professional skills and knowledge.
- Remains calm and professional under pressure, defusing conflict and being prepared to step forward and take control when required.

Professionalism is a challenging competency. This is mainly on the basis that in a true competency frame working programme, the description applied to this would not be acceptable. There is quite simply far too many aspects and "competencies" to roll into one given scenario to achieve the overall description of "Professionalism". Not only are the Police Service looking for you to demonstrate courage, resilience and being able to act on your own initiative, they are looking for your honesty, integrity and you respect for race and diversity. You must be able to challenge unprofessional or discriminatory behaviour as well as asking for feedback and learning from this. Finally the ability to defuse volatile situations and take personal responsibility for the situation are also included in this Core Competency.

Decision making

- Gathers, verifies and assesses all appropriate and available information to gain an accurate understanding of situations.
- Considers a range of possible options before making clear, timely, justifiable decisions.
- Reviews decisions in the light of new information and changing circumstances.
- Balances risks, costs and benefits, thinking about the wider impact of decisions.
- Exercises discretion and applies professional judgement, ensuring actions and decisions are proportionate and in the public interest.

In direct paradox to Professionalism, Decision Making is a very clearly and well defined description of a key skill all good Police Officers retain. A vast proportion of your role as a Police Constable is based on your ability to make quick and timely decisions based on justification and your discretionary powers.

Working with others

- Works co-operatively with others to get things done, willingly giving help and support to colleagues.
- Is approachable, developing positive working relationships.
- Explains things well, focusing on the key points and talking to people using language they understand.
- Listens carefully and asks questions to clarify understanding, expressing own views positively and constructively.
- Persuades people by stressing the benefits of a particular approach, keeps them informed of progress and manages their expectations.
- Is courteous, polite and considerate, showing empathy and compassion.
- Deals with people as individuals and addresses their specific needs and concerns.
- Treats people with respect and dignity, dealing with them fairly and without prejudice regardless of their background or circumstances.

Don't be drawn into the title of this particular Core Competency. Whilst working with others would normally translate to Team Work, there is far more to this competency, including your ability to communicate effectively with others, persuasion skills and the ability to treat all people with respect and dignity. Again this relates to an absolute requirement for all Police Officers to have respect for race and diversity.

CHAPTER 3 THE INTERACTIVE EXERCISES

F or the vast proportion of candidates, the role play section of the one day assessment centre is probably one of the most daunting tasks. Certainly from the feedback I have received over the last seven years of delivering training on how to pass this process, candidates lose the greatest amount of confidence when preparing for the interactive exercises. In this chapter, you will discover some useful and confidence building techniques, along with practical advice which has assisted in numerous candidates scoring very highly at the assessment centre.

Each of the four exercises are broken down into two components. The Preparation Phase and The Activity Phase (when you actually enter a room and meet the role play actor). All of the information about The Westshire ® Centre is sent to you in advance and you are to use this, along with the brief provided to you in the Preparation Phase, to formulate your plan for the Activity Phase.

Before You Attend The Day

A great deal of people who attended on one of our courses, turned up with their copy of The Westshire ® Centre information pack, much of it with scribbles and notes or huge highlighted sections of information that they believe is relevant.

Here is a huge hint **"Don't try and remember it all"**

Why? Well simply because there is too much information to take in! You will be placed into an unnatural and stressful situation, accessing your memory powers and normal working processes will be greatly hindered by this. So what information should you retain? What is useful and relevant?

In this section of this book, I would really encourage you to do every step of the following process.

Building A Relevant Memory Tool

Do you have a perfect memory? Probably not you will probably be thinking. But, I am sure you can recall significant past events, situations or emotionally charged occurrences from your distant past. Why? How does your brain recall these events with absolute clarity, yet filters out loads of other memories so that they become clouded and vague?

Think of your brain as a super computer, searching through all the files on its hard drive, looking for reference points to an event. The more relevant reference points to a particular folder and file, the easier it is for the computer to locate the information, retrieve it and display it on the screen, your memory.

Let's consider how we all experience the world, it's through our senses of Sight, Sound, Feel, Taste all linked with Emotional Response. Think of these as the data input to your memory file and also reference points when your brain decides to store away the experience. It makes sense then that, the greater the number of reference points, with absolute detail and linked data, the easier it is to retrieve at a later date.

We learn and experience the world through our senses. What is really interesting is that there are variations in people as to which sense or learning/language style we prefer. Some are Visual people, using sight as a predominant learning experience. Some people are Auditory people, where music or sound has a greater influence on them and so on.

I assume, I haven't met you yet, unless you will have been on one of our fantastic one day courses where we have great fun, getting this firmly stuck in your memory, for you to use at the assessment centre. Follow this process and I promise you, having bumped into previous course attendees a year or two later, it will still be accessible from your memory.

First off, let us put the fictitious retail and leisure complex into a familiar context.

In a moment, I would like you to close your eyes and think about your local, regional shopping centre. Somewhere like, Bluewater in Kent or The Oracle in Reading or the Bull Ring in Birmingham. Hopefully you have visited somewhere like this.

Think about walking around the mall areas, the sounds, the lights, the colour of the flooring, how busy it is on a Saturday morning with families and others around.

Close your eyes for just 2 minutes and think about it so that it is crystal clear in your mind.

Done it? Make sure you have before you move on, no cheating here, it won't help you!

Assuming you have let's move on.

That place you remembered and walked around in your minds eye, is from now on called "The Westshire ® Centre". When thinking about the centre, visualise that place to give you mental context of the environment. For the purpose of the Interactive Exercises and Written Exercises, you have to believe you work there, so immerse yourself in that role.

Grab a spare piece of paper and a pen!!

The description of the centre states that it has 2 floors so draw 2 parallel horizontal lines like below on your piece of paper. Spread them out a bit more than this.

These are to remind you that the centre has two floors. Why, because if you enter a role play and don't ask the relevant questions, eg **"where did you last see this gentleman, was he upstairs or downstairs?"** you may miss some important information.

The centre is described as having numerous car parking spaces and disabled parking bays for disabled badge holders, it has good transportation links to many nearby towns and villages etc. There are 156 shops and blah blah. Much of this is irrelevant, because if you visualise your local regional shopping centre, do you know, *"how many car parking spaces there are?"* No! *"Do you know all of its transport links?"* Probably not. *"Do you know how many shops are in the centre?"* No!

Discard all of this as it's not a priority to remember.

Do remember that <u>"Wheelchairs are available for free, from the main customer services desk"</u>

This will form an important part of your memory tool creation.

Back to our memory tool.

<u>"Downstairs in the middle of the centre is the Food Court where there is a Bar"</u>. This is important to remember as a bar is where alcoholic beverages are served and alcohol can equal trouble.

Add these two your memory tool.

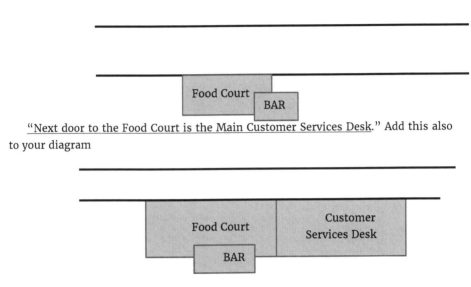

"Next door to the Food Court is the Main Customer Services Desk." Add this also to your diagram

"Wheelchairs are available for free from the Main Customer Services Desk".
Why is this relevant? Well wheelchairs are normally required by people with some form of Medical condition or ailment. This helps you link the next items together.

"The centre has a Medical Centre, staffed by a Registered Nurse and other qualified first aiders"
Knowing this is extremely useful for the role plays if given a scenario which may contain an injured or potentially injured person that needs attention. Add the Medical Centre to your diagram.

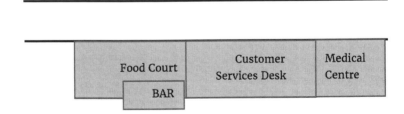

There are a number of teams that also work in the centre, these can be used as part of the broader role play scenarios, to assist you in your resolutions to potential issues.

Housekeeping – There are a number of housekeepers in the centre who are there to maintain tidiness and cleanliness of the facilities. These people are useful for SPILLS or MESS which represent a safety hazard to you, members of the public or other staff members.

Security Team – At any one time there are 8 -20 security guards on duty, for the protection and health and safety of customers and visitors to the centre. Remember that 8 is also the same number of CCTV cameras dotted around the centre. CCTV can be used for all sorts of activities.

Police Officers – 2 Police Officers are present in the centres own Police Station, which is manned only when the centre is open. They are there for any serious problems, such as crimes etc.

Drawn these three teams on your diagram so that it now looks like this.

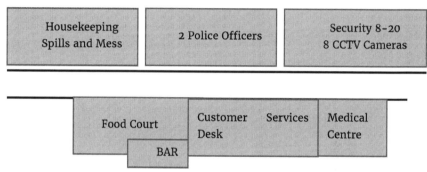

Your main duties and responsibilities as a Customer Services Officer are all directly linked to the 6 Core Competencies of a Police Officer. This page in the document should be recognised as such and matching the two roles should be easily realised.

Importantly, in your role as a Customer Services Officer, you "do not supervise staff". This scenario setting remember, is directly linked to the role of a Police Constable, not a Sergeant or Inspector with management responsibilities.

Within the information pack sent to you, there is one bullet point of particular importance. It states:

- Making announcements over the tannoy

This innocuous little sentence is actually exceptionally important to you and your success in some of the potential role plays you may face. Using the tannoy is your means of involving other members of the greater team, in assisting you in the given scenario.

There will be no actual "tannoy" system for you to use, instead, consider explaining your thought process and what you would do, to the role play actor.

For example, the role play actor states that there is a situation in the centre whereby an elderly lady was surrounded by a group of youths after she slipped on the wet floor. Whilst she was on the floor it is believed that she was injured and the youths set about taking her purse.

Here is how to utilise the tannoy.

First explain that the lady's injuries are your priority and that the centre has a Medical Centre, staffed by a trained nurse who can administer first aid. After confirming the location of the lady state "I'm just going to use the tannoy to ask the nurse to go to that location to help the lady"

You briefly turn to one side, breaking eye contact with the role play actor and then state "Ok, I've done that now, help is on its way." You can then expand on this by using the rest of the team EG:

"You say that this lady slipped over on the wet floor, that's very concerning as it will also represent a trip hazard to other customers and staff, I will inform the Housekeeping Team to attend and clear that up. Also, this group of youths have allegedly committed a crime so I will contact the two Police Officers and our Security Team, to have them tracked down and investigated appropriately, I will just get those teams in action using the tannoy. Ok, I have done that and they are on their way. Please give me more information on......."

When running our One Day Training Courses, some people would state they are nervous about explaining the use of a tannoy. You are essentially acting and people also feel uncomfortable about this. Please try not to as this skill set is no different to the role of a Police Officer. Consider this, whilst out on patrol as a fully-fledged serving Police Officer, you come across a road traffic collision. A motorcyclist has been killed, along with one occupant of a motor vehicle which is on it's roof. You are the first on scene and the driver of the car is alive and conscious but trapped an in considerable pain. Naturally you will ensure your own safety before approaching the scene etc, but then you would probably attend to this last surviving casualty. I would suggest that the conversation would go along the lines of

"Please try to remain calm, I can see you are in pain and I want to get help here as quickly as possible. I am just going to use my *RADIO* to contact the Fire Brigade and the Ambulance services so that we can get you out and looked after....."

Or words to that effect.

Your tannoy at the One Day Assessment Centre is the equivalent to a serving Police Officer's radio. Don't be afraid to use it! Now add it to your memory picture like so:

YOU CAN DOWNLOAD YOUR FREE COPY OF THE MEMORY TOOL BY VISITING WWW.MONEYTREEMASTERS.CO.UK AND SIGNING UP TO OUR EXCLUSIVE FREE BONUS MATERIAL LIST – A LINK WILL BE SENT TO YOU.

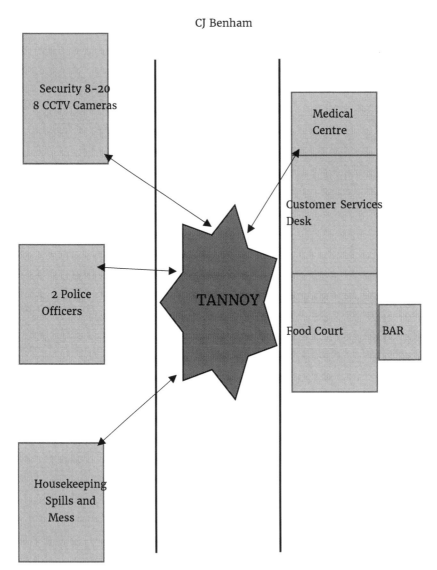

Equality Policy Statement

The centres Equality Policy Statement is a reference to pure respect for race and diversity. Updated in approximately 2014 to keep up with more prominent equality legislation the EPS is there to protect both staff, customers and visitors to the centre. Essentially you must ensure that no one breeches this statement whilst in the role play EG; use offensive or derogatory language about someone's age, sex, sexual orientation, gender reassignment, race, religion or belief, disability, marriage and civil partnership or pregnancy and maternity. This applies to discrimination and or harassment.

Harassment includes any unwanted conduct (including words, behaviour or a combination of both) directed at person on the basis of any of the above mentioned factors, which has the purpose or effect of violating their dignity or creating an intimidating, hostile, degrading, humiliating or offensive environment.

The centre does not tolerate discrimination or harassment of any kind.

It is important for you to have a good understanding of this and the three steps outlined in the complaints procedure for The Westshire ® Centre. These three steps are

A – Ask the other person to stop. This means someone may not be doing something with the intention of discriminating the victim or harassing them. If they are asked to stop what they are doing and they comply, then the matter needs to go no further

B- Talk to an appropriate person about the situation to establish if there is discrimination or harassment. Guess who this person will be? Yes, it will be YOU the Customer Services Officer.

C- Complain in writing to the centres Operations Manager who will investigate the situation and take the appropriate actions.

Add the Equality Policy Statement to your memory picture like so:

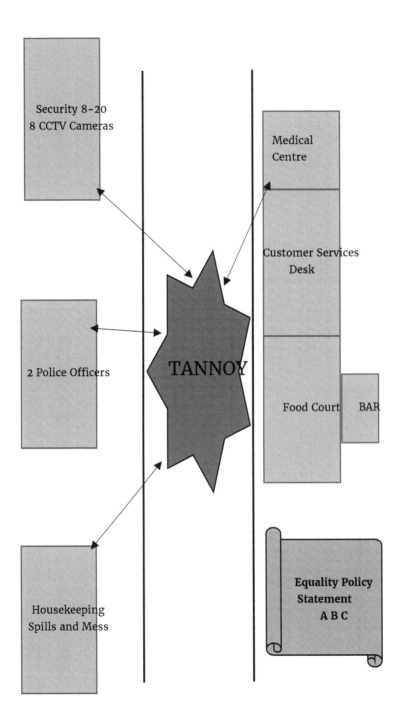

Code of Conduct

The centres Code of Conduct is basically a list of do's and don'ts. Most of these are relatively common sense EG; not misusing escalators, blocking walkways or using offensive language or behaving antisocially. If anyone is found to be not abiding with the code, then the centre reserves the right to escort them away from the premises and ban them if appropriate. Remember, if someone uses foul or offensive language in the role play, you **must** challenge it firmly but appropriately.

Add this to the diagram.

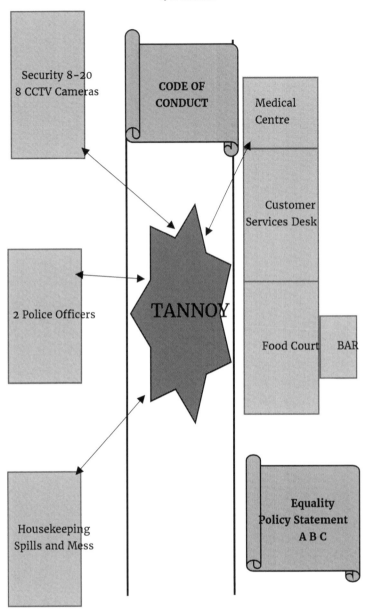

IMPORTANT UPDATE - 2017: The police service have now introduced an additional document into the Westshire Centre structure. This is termed Standards of Performance and Ethics. This new set of guidelines will effect your role plays and the future assessment centres – pay particular attention to anything new is my advice!

The Westshire Standards of Performance and Ethics effects all members of the Westshire Centre staff and relates to the following key principles.

Integrity –

- You must always act in the interest of customers.
- You must provide a high level of service.
- You must challenge /report improper language or behaviour from colleagues or customers in an appropriate manner.

Fairness –

- You must treat everyone fairly regardless of age, gender, ethnicity or any other personal characteristic.
- You must not act in ways which are biased or prejudiced for or against others.

Respect –

- You must show respect to both colleagues and customers regardless of the situation.
- You must use language appropriately and sensitively with others.

Honesty –

- You must be honest in your interactions with people.
- You must clarify any ambiguities and not misrepresent any facts when dealing with colleagues or customers.

Now that your memory tool is complete, practice it and learn it. You should ensure you are able to draw all of these elements and link them together. Why is this so important? Well something on this diagram will be able to assist you in 99% of the role plays that the One Day Assessment Centre can through at you.

Try to remember it with the following paragraph.

"The centre has 2 floors, downstairs in the middle is the food court, where there is a bar. Next door to this is the Customer Services Desk, where you can get wheelchairs for free. Wheelchairs reminded me of a medical condition and that the centre also has a Medical Centre, staffed by a nurse. He/She is useful for first aid. There are also a Housekeeping Team, useful for spills and mess, a Security Team, 8 - 20 of them and 8 reminds me that there are also 8 CCTV cameras around the centre. There are also 2 Police Officers and I can get hold of all of these people using the TANNOY. The centre operates under an Equality Policy Statement, which has 3 steps, ASK them to stop, Come and see ME and finally to COMPLAIN in writing.

Alongside the Equality Policy Statement, there is also a Code of Conduct. I must at all times abide by the Statement of Performance and Ethics – Integrity, Fairness, Respect and Honesty"

Draw the diagram, repeat the words. Draw it again and continue to repeat the process until you have it firmly lodged in your mind. This way, when you attend the assessment centre, as part of your preparation for each role play. You will be able to note this diagram down and use it to your advantage.

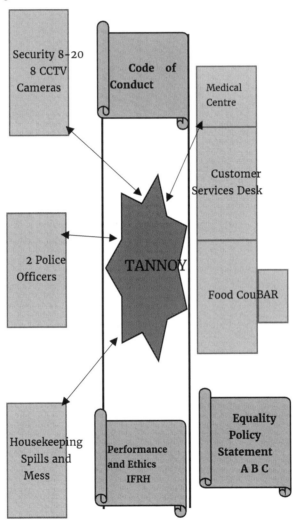

CHAPTER 4 THE DIFFERENT PHASES OF THE INTERACTIVE EXERCISES

The role play scenarios are each split into two phases. Time is allocated evenly for each section and there are just a few short moments between each exercise to compose yourself and go again for the next one.

The Preparation Phase

The first part of each role play is when you are given 5 minutes to prepare and study an information brief. You are allowed to make notes and take these into the role play with you. The briefs are normally quite long but not overly detailed. Try not to fall into the trap of planning how you will handle the situation. That probably seems counter intuitive, to NOT plan. However, it has been proven time and time again that candidates that enter the Activity Phase of the scenario, go into the room, with a structured plan that is almost instantly rendered useless by the brief that the role play actor has been given. My advice to all candidates is "don't plan". Make some key notes and draw the memory tool diagram. Go into the situation like you would today in your day job. For example, very few people who, will be told that there is a complaining customer that needs attention, sit down and "plan" the conversation:

"I will say this and he will probably say that. Then I will do this and he will do that...."

Most people take the initial brief of information, extract key information then go to the customer and say "How can I help?" Then react to the customer appropriately. Too often, when placed in role play scenarios people will think and plan too much. Be natural and confident in your own abilities.

The Activity Phase

In the Activity Phase you will enter the room and meet the role play actor, normally they are seated. There will also be an Assessor in the room. Don't worry about this person, remain focused on the role play actor. When you enter the room, have something to say. That is, don't enter the room and be blithering or uncertain how to start the conversation. Try;

"Hi, my name is.............. I am the Customer Services Officer, how can I help you?"

Don't offer your hand for a handshake, it won't be accepted and you will be left standing with your arm outstretched and feeling a little deflated.

Use questions, lots of them! Questions are your friends and a skilled questioner will be able to extract more or hidden information that the role play actor may have been brief to retain unless asked numerous times.

Open questions have who, where, what, why, when or how at the start. These are great for conversation or topic openers.

"Okay, please tell me how this happened?"

"Why do you think this happened?"

Closed questions can clarify a position and have only an alternative answer, A or B.

"Was his shirt a long sleeve (A) or a short sleeve (B) design?"

Try to remember that not all role plays have a solution, it may be that the role play actor's brief is to decline any suggestions you make or to reject any recommendations. You can of course ask them for their suggestions but, you will probably find they will decline to provide any. Select your best course of action and pursue this as the strategy for moving the situation going forwards.

Police Officer role play actors tend to be seated nowadays, and the scenarios are never violent or overly threatening, so relax and expect some low level hostility but nothing that would cause you harm or severe distress. From the feedback I have received from numerous sources, the majority of role plays are based on equality and respect for diversity. This fits in with the Equality Policy Statement and if the role play actor uses offensive or derogatory language, you must challenge it!

To challenge inappropriate or offensive language you should employ a technique I call a "Requested Order". This is not as direct as saying to someone;

"You can't say that" or "Don't say things like that". These could come across as antagonistic or argumentative, in any case too forceful. On the flip side you need to be strong than just saying "Please don't say things like that".

A Requested Order uses tonality of voice and specific language to turn a request into an order. Here is the language;

"Please refrain from using derogatory terms or offensive language. We don't tolerate that here at the Westshire Centre. Please, just stick to the facts. Is that okay?"

Tonality is a little tricky to convey in a book but emphasis and assertiveness need to be translated in the phrasing above for the request to evolve into an order.

""Please *refrain from using derogatory terms or offensive language*. **We don't tolerate that here** at the Westshire Centre. **Please, just stick to the facts**. Is that okay?"

The italics would represent assertiveness, the bold underlined sections more force in your tonality and phrasing.

CHAPTER 5 PRE-CIRCULATED ROLE PLAY SCENARIO INFORMATION

I n the pre-circulated information provided in the joining instructions for the SEARCH One Day Assessment, you will be furnished very vague and brief explanations about the interactive exercises. The document will tend to provide the last names of the role play actors character, for example;

- Gamer, a shop owner in the centre, wants to discuss an incident that recently happened in the centre.
- Kowalski, a shop owner in the centre who wants to discuss an incident in their shop.
- Swift, a member of the community has asked for a meeting at the centre.
- Zajak, a business owner in the centre, who wants to discuss an incident in their shop.

As you can see these give nothing away in advance of attending. The full briefs at the assessment centre are also still fairly vague but provide a little more substance to the nature of the meeting you are about to enter.

In the past, scenarios have been varied and could include:

- Helping a parent who has lost their child
- Discussing a member of staff's continued lateness
- Discussing a group or particular ethnicity with a shop owner who he/she believes is trouble
- A member of the public complaining about security officers who work at the centre

- A shop owner who is not happy a security officer has not been present or left their post and something happened

Ensure you are using your ears more than your mouth. Sometimes you have to listen very carefully to the role play actor to work out what they ARE saying and more importantly what they are NOT saying! Small comments and vague responses should arouse your curiosity, follow it through and explore every small detail.

CHAPTER 6 HOW TO HANDLE COMPLAINING PEOPLE

B elow is a technique which is used to provide great customer service, discover why people are complaining and enables the introduction of possible remedies or solutions. If you are faced with a complaint follow this format and you won't go far wrong.

L

Listen to the complainant, genuinely! Use body language like nodding the head and smiling to show you are listening. Say things like "Yes, okay, I understand, go on"

A

Acknowledge their problem. This is where you get to demonstrate empathy and shoehorn in loads of Core Competency type phrases. "I can understand why you are upset by this, I would probably feel the same if I was in your shoes" "Here at the centre, we want to deliver the best customer service possible" "We are a very community based centre and want to ensure everyone feels included..."

P

Probe the problem. This is where you have to start using your questioning skills to establish the root cause of the problem. Most people will complain at a very high level with a broad statement. "Your shopping centre is bloody awful!" You need to drill down into the problem and find out exactly what has caused that perspective. Once you have completed this and you feel you have isolated it, you can move on.

S

Sidestep the root cause. Say something like "Ok, let's put that issue to one side for a second. Are you happy with X, and have you been pleased with Y......" Your tactic here is to get the person to start confirming everything else is okay or good. Once you have got a few yes's move back to the root issue and say "So if I could provide you with a solution to this area (the root cause), everything would be okay?" Now if they say "Yes" congratulations you definitely found your root cause. If however they say "No", circle back around to Probe and start again as you missed something.

CHAPTER 7 10 TOP TIPS FOR THE INTERACTIVE EXERCISES

1. Use the memory diagram. Draw it on a very small piece of paper that fits in the palm of your hand and take it into every role play. Something on there will help you
2. Don't plan how the conversation will pan out, you will be wrong. Make notes of the pertinent information on the back of your memory diagram. You can always refer to it in the activity phase
3. Have something to say when entering the room. "Hi, my name is.............. I am the Customer Services Officer, how may I help you?" Be confident and assertive but not arrogant or threatening
4. Listen carefully to the role play actor, act on what they do and sometimes do not say. If something is unclear, question it
5. Questions are your friends. Use them in abundance
6. Introduce as many keywords and phrases from the Core Competencies are possible to score higher
7. Don't assume you will be able to resolve the problem
8. Use requested orders rather than direct orders
9. Recap information with the role play actor to clarify your understanding of what has been said and their understanding of your proposals
10. Don't be afraid to use the team around you via introducing the Tannoy technique

CHAPTER 8 FINAL THOUGHTS

I hope you have found this guide useful and informative. Once again I would like to stress that information is not the key to success. Yes it helps, but having tactics and a strategy you can use, repeat and model success upon, is far more important.

We used to offer one day training courses for people who were serious about becoming Police Officers but stopped this practice as it was only focused on one geographical area and was becomingly increasingly expensive for candidates. This prevented a number of candidates from attending and benefitting from our knowledge and experience.

Our unique online course offers unrivalled access to all our materials, delivered by our lead tutor and included additional hints and tips. Once you subscribe to the course, all of the materials are available to you 24/7, 365 days a year, **for life**. Most importantly, you don't have to travel, pay for a hotel or the large cost of attending a one day course. We also don't charge and ongoing fee! It's just a single payment which I'm sure you will agree represents excellent value for money.

One high quality course, at a very good single price. Please do take a look and gain further information and tactics from our lead tutor and founder.

Be safe and good luck in your career.

CJ Benham
Founder of PasstheProcess and MoneyTreeMasters.

Please don't forget to leave your feedback on Amazon.

ONLINE COURSE AVAILABLE
Don't waste £'s or your valuable time attending an <u>expensive one day course</u>.
Sit back, relax and gain expert information, at your own pace and with the
ability to review and recap all elements of the course 24/7
<u>www.moneytreemasters.co.uk</u>

**Sign Up on the Link on the page to get your free Memory Tool Download and
exclusive FREE additional content.**

16328538R00023

Printed in Great Britain
by Amazon